To my wife, Yvonne, for her willingness to read and listen to ALL of my poems, and give valued criticism; a noble sacrifice indeed!

Thanks, also, to all of the folk who have shared so many stories with me, their input is much appreciated.

A special thanks to Kath Helm, who has been the source of a number of poems, and always good for a story!

Australian Poems that would Flummox a FARMER

Philip R. Rush

By the same author

Bess, The Black Orpington Swaggie
Australian Poems That Would Stun A Sheep
More Than Nine Lives
Australian Poems That Would Boggle A Bull
Tales from Mosquito Gully and Other Australian Poems
Aussie Poems for Gnome and Garden

Published by Philip R. Rush Pty. Ltd. A.C.N. 082 969 882
224 Sunny Hills Road
Glen Huon Tasmania 7109

Copyright © text Philip R. Rush 1998
Copyright © illustrations Syd Woon 1999

1st Edition   March 1998   4000 copies
2nd Reprint   June 1999   3000 copies
3rd Reprint   July 2000   3000 copies

Printed and bound by The Monotone Art Printers Pty Ltd.
Argyle Street, Hobart Tasmania

ISBN   0 9585443 5 2

CONTENTS

AN AUSSIE CHRISSIE

(Australians have a habit of shortening many of the words they use, and adding the "ie" sound to the shortened or complete word. Words such as 'mosquito', 'football', and 'university' are spoken of as 'mossie', 'footy', and 'uni'.
These abbreviations are sometimes hard for other Australians to follow, let alone people from other countries!
This poem includes some of the many common shortened forms of words Australians use in everyday speech.)

We had a marvellous Chrissie, we all had heaps of pressies,
I bought Janelle's and Robbie's, and Timothy's and Dessie's:
I bought Barbies for the missies, and teddies for the twinnies,
And for the wife, who watches birds, a brand new pair of
   binnies.

We invited lots of people; our neighbours June and Lockie,
Jenny and her hubby came, and Sammy came from Rocky.
Rellies came from everywhere, from Tassie and from Brissie,
And Hughie came from Berri, along with Auntie Lizzie.

We had Tommy, he's a chalkie, and Jimmy who's a chippie;
And even nephew Barry, who's a greenie and a hippie!
He's a little airy-fairy, but I don't think he's a druggie,
Which I couldn't say for certain of our wharfie, Uncle Dougie!

We got them all together to take a Chrissie pickie,
And it wasn't all that simple, it was really very tricky!
Some were feeling cranky, and some were drinking coldies,
And some didn't want a pickie, especially the oldies!

In the arvo we played footy, but Johnny did his hammy,
And Tommy strained his quaddie, so we had a double
    whammy!
So we took to playing cricket, and I had a go at Greggie,
And I must have bowled like Warnie, for I got him with a
    leggie!

The youngsters went off swimming, all those that brought their
    cossies;
Went swimming in the river, but they couldn't stand the
    mossies.
So they came back rather early, and some of them played
    tiggy,
While a couple of the nephews stayed behind to have a ciggy.

We had an evening barbie, and the sausages were crummy,
But the steaks were extra specky, and the yabbies, they were
    yummy!
I reckon we had fifty folks, including friends and rellies,
Not counting all the kiddies, who were inside watching telly.

When the meat had all been eaten we had plates of cheese and
    bikkies,
(Which didn't suit Aunt Lizzie who was always rather picky!)
We finished off the barbie with some tinnies and some
    stubbies,
While the littlies watched the programme of their favourite
    Teletubbies.

All around the barbie things were looking pretty messy,
So I called my kelpies over, that's Blackie, Jock, and Jessie.
They ate up all the goodies, the mushies, bones and taties,
They even ate a Wellie that I think was sister Katie's!

Now Johnny, he's from Tassie, had to catch a plane to Lonnie,
So he left a little early with my other brother, Ronnie.
On the way, a drunken truckie, who was only known as Bluey,
Missed a turn-in off the highway, and he tried to do a u-ey!

Now Ronnie's not a weakie, he spun the wheel, and nearly
Ran off the road completely as he did a specky wheelie!
And a bikie who was following said, "You were very lucky;
It was nearly goodnight granny thanks to Blue, the alkie
        truckie!

The party was a doozy, not a single stoush or barney,
(Except when Kevvie argued with his next-door neighbour,
        Arnie).
But, hooley-dooley, it was exie, we spent a heap of lolly,
Next year we'll fly to Straddie for a sunny, Chrissie hollie!

binnies - binoculars   *u-ey - a 'U-turn' when driving*
Rocky - Rockhampton   *specky - special, spectacular*
chalkie - schoolteacher   *alkie - an alcoholic*
chippie - carpenter   *bikie - a motor-bike rider*
pickie - picture   *cossie - swimming costumes*
exie - expensive   *wheelie - a skid*
coldies - chilled beer   *Straddie - Stradbroke Island*
Wellie - rubber gumboot   *Lonnie - Launceston*
Warnie - Shane Warne, famous Australian cricketer
leggie - leg-break, to bowl a ball that turns sharply on landing

THE GELDING

(The Tasmanian Carriage Drivers' Association celebrated their twenty-fifth anniversary in January, 1999. I was asked to write a poem for the occasion, and was given both the title, and the name of the horse that features in these verses.
Since being somewhat ignorant of the particular subject matter, I was also given a little bit of background information, and was able to come up with the following, which was apparently received very well at the Carriage Drivers' Association's Anniversary!)

A dashing young stallion and handsome was I,
With a flair for the fillies and fire in my eye;
I had my own paddock for two years or more,
And I lived very well, for the mares were next door!
They'd look at me longingly hour after hour,
And stand there agog at my strength and my power.
I'd play up a treat; kick my heels in the air,
Show off what I had to all of them there.
I'd gallop about, I'd rear up on high,
There never was stallion as manly as I!

This life, I had reckoned, was too good to last.
I was harnessed one day, and my freedom was past.
I was taught how to walk, I was taught how to trot,
When to lift up my legs, and when I should not.
I was taught how to pull, bend my neck at the poll;
A show-ring career for me was their goal.
A rusty, old jog-cart, while still on the farm,
Was the first thing I pulled, yet it did me no harm.
I soon was adept and they took me to town,
And I did very well, both up hill and down.

I resented this training but, after a while,
I learned I was good, had an excellent style.
In fact, I was great, all the people would clap
As I passed in a cart, or a carriage, or trap.
I enjoyed the attention, I held my head high,
And soon the resentment was gone from my eye.
I played to the crowds that I passed in the street,
And kept a strict rhythm with all of my feet.
And then, I remember, a long time ago,
Out came the carriage to use for the Show!

My very first Show! It was not very grand:
It had, I'll admit, a Scottish Pipe Band;
But nothing much else; I think that I won
As the best harness horse - I guess it was fun.
But bigger and grander was still yet to be,
And the better the Show, the better I'd be!
I won ribbons a-plenty, I won ribbons galore,
But still all I wanted was to win even more.
Oh! I still loved the fillies, I still loved the mares,
And enjoyed their respect at all of the fairs!

But then came disaster! I suppose it was spring;
I misbehaved badly, I did the wrong thing.
I was drawing a carriage at some fancy Show
When I saw this young filly with get up and go.
So I got up and went, and the filly came, too,
And this caused an uproar, a hullabaloo!
My master was livid! I felt pretty good,
Doing the things that young horses should.
But Master thought different - "You've caused enough strife!
It's home for you, lad, and out with the knife!"

I kept winning prizes; my high-stepping gait
Won ribbons at home, and fame Interstate.
But my interest in fillies had dwindled somewhat,
And I scarce gave a glance as they passed at a trot.
I might sometimes have said, "Girls, have a good day."
But I no longer cared to wander or stray.
My name, in the show-ring, when young, fit and healthy,
Was Mountain View, something, Paluka Adelphi.
But not any more; and, just now and then,
My Master will call me - a plain, simple "Ben."

I trot over to see him - well, that isn't true,
I walk rather stiffly, that's all I can do.
I have my own paddock down here on the flat,
But no mares or fillies, there's no more of that!
My Master will stroke me, and then go away,
I mightn't then see him the rest of the day.
So I stand in my paddock, I stand and I dream
Of being the Champ of a great carriage team.
And sometimes, just sometimes, I heave a huge sigh,
And think of days past with a tear in my eye!

PIGGY JOHNSON

(This story was told to me by a fellow living in a small country town in Victoria. He guaranteed that it was true, for he knew the bloke I have called Piggy Johnson in this poem.
However, this wasn't the first time I had heard similar stories, the only differences being the name of the town and the characters.
Another rural myth, perhaps?

I came to town one morning from my camp out in the scrub,
And met this filthy fellow inside the local pub.
They called him Piggy Johnson, for he rarely took a bath,
And his motor-bike was idling, unattended, on the path.

"Is that your bike still purring on the path beside the gate?"
And Piggy nodded sagely, "I keep 'er runnin', mate;
For I find it 'ard to start 'er when she's been at rest a while.
I'd hate to push 'er 'ome from 'ere, it's close to seven mile!"

I bought this bloke a drink or two, then chatted on some more.
"Is that your dog beside the bike that I observed before?"
"He's one of three or four I 'ave, 'e 'appens to be Blue;
And 'e, like all the others 'ave, 'as earned a quid or two."

I looked a little mystified, but Piggy said no more,
He'd seen a stranger to the town come wandering through the
        door.
He watched the bloke for quite a while, then sauntered to the
        bar.
"I've not seen you before, me man; you come from near or
        far?"

"I'm only passing through, me lad, I'm heading home today;
I won't be here for very long, I live up Queensland way."
"Uh-huh," said Piggy Johnson, "Can I offer you a drink?"
And, as he did, he turned to me and gave a knowing wink.

I didn't have a lot to do, so stayed and watched a while
As Piggy played him like a trout with all his native guile.
It only took a drink or two before the stranger said,
"Yeah, I might buy that dog of yours you say is Kelpie bred."

As they left the pub together, I followed on behind;
I have, as you can plainly see, an investigative mind.
Not wanting to look obvious, I sat upon a seat
That stood beside the hotel door, and faced the busy street.

Now Piggy spun this bloke a yarn, in accents clear and loud,
That would have done that writer chap, old William
        Shakespeare, proud.
He acted out his sorry tale with drama, style and verve,
I didn't think that Piggy would have had that sort of nerve!

He certainly convinced the chap his dog was quite the best.
"Try 'im out right now," he said. "He'll manage any test."
"I haven't time," the stranger said. "But, yes, I'll purchase
        Blue.
How much you want?" And Pig replied, "A 'undred bucks 'll
        do."

"That's cheap for such a champion dog, but, as I said before,
I can't, because of failin' 'ealth, keep any dogs no more."
This Queensland bloke, he sympathised, but Piggy said,
     "That's life!
You don't live out yer years on earth without some sort of
     strife."

He picked Blue up and placed him in the Queensland
     stranger's ute;
He gave the dog a fond farewell; he was a devious coot!

The fellow paid his hundred bucks and headed on his way,
But not before old Piggy had another word to say.

The stranger got inside his cab and switched the engine on,
In just another moment he'd be out of town and gone;
But Piggy stood beside the tray, and then to Bluey said
A word or two in undertones, and pat him on the head.

He watched the ute head up the road, then went back through
     the door
To have another drink or two, and then a couple more.
He left just shy of closing time, rode out along the track,
But blow me down! Next afternoon both he and Blue were
     back!

"How come you've got your dog again?" Old Piggy looked at
     me,
And said, a twinkle in his eye, "It's just like this, you see;
The road that leads folk out of town goes right past Piggy's
     shack,
And it's a steepish bit of road, a windin' bit o' track."

"A double bend's beside my place, you 'ave to take it slow,
And Blue is not a stupid dog, as you and I well know.
'Home, Blue!' was what I said to 'im as that bloke drove away,
And so I found 'im home last night; that's why 'e's back
     today!"

"I put the dog into the ute, I 'ad to 'ave 'im free,
And, once the bloke was safely in, I told 'im 'Home!' yer see.
I've sold old Blue a dozen times, 'e's just that sort o' dog,
And, as yer see, 'e does me well by payin' for me grog!"

EARTHWORMS

(A tribute to some of our unseen workers!
Just a little aside! One of the small country schools where I
was Headteacher was in the middle of a dairying district. The
schoolground itself did not have the best soil, but we dug up
three separate square yards of ground, counted the earthworms
in each plot, and worked out how many worms altogether in
the schoolyard.
The homework for that night was to do the same on each of
their farms - and the result was that the ten or eleven properties
had enough worms to stretch, head to tail, from the earth to the
moon and back!!)

Have you ever thought about the fact that every little worm
Is busy ploughing up our fields with every twist and squirm?
From dawn to dusk they work away and, maybe, through the
     night;
For chomping through our tons of soil to them is pure delight.

Not only do they plough our fields, they fertilise as well,
Although they never leave behind a fertiliser smell.
They live just inches underground in every type of soil,
And every farmer benefits from earthworms' ceaseless toil.

There's many mightn't realise how many worms they've got
Wriggling underneath their farms but, surely, there's a lot!
With only ten worms to the yard, this fact should raise a smile,
A hundred acres' worth of worms would stretch three hundred
     mile!

SILVER AND GOLD

(One doesn't have to have a lot of money to be rich!)
I never was a wealthy man in terms of pounds and pence,
But I'm surrounded all about by riches quite immense.
I live in the Australian Bush upon a mountainside,
And feast on many treasures that to others are denied.

I don't own bags of diamonds, or rubies rich and rare,
But, as I look around me, there's riches everywhere!
The wattle in profusion blooms, a waving sea of gold;
And jewel-ed clouds at sunset are a wonder to behold!

No cellar underneath our house has bottles full of wine,
But, on our forty-acre block, I see the water shine
As, in the broken shadows, it tumbles through the trees,
A creek of purest water, a treasure-trove to me!

No chest of golden sovereigns or fortune I possess,
And million-dollar paintings I'll never own, I guess;
But priceless are the landscapes that I see every day,
Mountains, rivers, forests - and not a cent to pay!

No cupboard full of silver is in my house, and yet
There's silver in abundance once the evening sun has set.
The river-mist reflects the moon in shades of pearly-white,
And silvered trees, and silver stars add to the magic night!

I've never been a wealthy man, not in the worldly sense,
But in my deck-chair I can sit, or lean against a fence
And gaze at riches of my own - the views I see each day,
And, precious though these treasures are, there's not a cent to
        pay!

"START OFF SLOW...."

(A friend of mine, a dear lady well into her eighties, has been the source for a number of my poems. She spent most of her life on a farm in rural Tasmania, and has told me many a tale and anecdote that I have found more than useful when I have been looking for something to write about!
A very hard worker all her life, she is now unable to work like she used to, but still does what she can.
I dropped into see her one day, after I had had a very hectic week. She offered me some advice, which I hand on to you in this poem!)

I've talked before of Auntie Kath, a lady I know well,
And she, who's now past eighty years, has many tales to tell.
She used to work from dawn to dusk, and sometimes even
      more,
"But now," she says in confidence, "when I reached eighty-
      four
I changed my attitude to work, for now I'm growing old;
My body won't obey my mind, it won't do as its told!
And so my motto now," she says, a twinkle in her eye,
"Is start off slow and slacken off; that's something you should
      try!"

Start off slow and slacken off! Those words helped me recall
A swaggie I met years ago, by name of Jackie Ball.
A bloke of undetermined age, with billy, swag, and pipe;
"I'm not," he said, "a working man - I'm not the working type.

I've travelled round this land of ours for nigh on fifty years,
I've done a bit of rousing, and sometimes used the shears.
But mostly I have managed to live my motto true,
'Start off slow and slacken off!' Now there's advice for you!"

'Start off slow and slacken off!' My neighbour's teenage son
Is driving his poor father mad, he never gets things done!
All through his schooling he had been a weary sort of lad,
Not violent or obnoxious, his behaviour wasn't bad.
But he just seemed to drift along, no homework did he do,
But even so, I don't know how, he managed to get through.
So now he's home upon the farm, I hear his father cry,
"You start off slow and slacken off! At least give work a try!"

'Start off slow and slacken off.' For Auntie Kath that's fine,
She's earned her latter years of rest, this dear old friend of
          mine.
She's laboured hard throughout her life, and now it's time to
          say,
"Start off slow and slacken off! I won't do much today."
But I have some advice to you, all those who care to hear,
I've learnt it through experience, and so these words sincere
I've written in this verse of mine for all of you to share -
To start off slow and slacken off won't get you anywhere!

A LOVER OF SCRUBBIN'

(Another poem about 'Auntie Kath'. My wife telephoned her one day, and, during the conversation, Kath mentioned that she was 'A lover of scrubbin' - hence this poem.)

"I'm a lover of scrubbin'," she said to my wife,
"A lover of scrubbin' I've been all my life!
When I was a littl'un I scrubbed all the floor,
And the steps that led up to our old wooden door.
I scrubbed our large table with soap every day,
I scrubbed it so hard I near wore it away!
Each Monday we washed, and I scrubbed all the clothes;
The buckets and copper, I also scrubbed those.
When we got linoleum I kept it so bright
By scrubbing it daily with all of my might!
And, now that I'm older, I still scrub today,
But I can't scrub in quite such a vigorous way."

My wife asked this octogenarian friend,
"You still find you're able to stretch and to bend
To scrub this and that?" And our friend said, "I must.
I still have to clean and I still have to dust.
I keep the sink sparkling, and my wood-heater, too,
I scrub the glass clean so the fire can shine through!
And not only that," she said, with a grin,
"I have, once a week, a cleaning girl in.
So I still have to scrub," she said to my spouse,
"For I'd hate her to find any dirt in the house!"

KEEPING TRACK

(There's no need for a lengthy introduction to this poem, sufficient to say that one needs to be sure to ask the implied question in the poem to someone with a sense of humour!)

I knew a bloke of ninety-odd, or somewhere thereabouts,
Who'd weathered many storms and floods, who'd faced his
      share of droughts;
His father ran a dairy farm amongst some rolling hills,
And Harold, that's the bloke I knew, inherited his skills.

There were no better farming chaps than Harold and his Dad,
They always managed very well in seasons good or bad.
The father started up the farm in eighteen eighty-three,
"And that's the farm where I was born," this Harold said to
      me.

"Dad started off with Ayrshire cows, and Dairy Shorthorns,
      too;
At least, that's what I think he had, and maybe just a few
Of Jerseys to top up the herd; but then, I can't be sure:
We changed across to Holsteins back in nineteen sixty-four."

I listened to him for a while, then innocently said,
"I think I've heard it said before, or, maybe, somewhere read
That years ago the farmers tied a home-made tinkling bell
Around the neck of cows and bulls; but why, I cannot tell."

Old Harold took the well-laid bait, and ventured on to say,
How farms had far less fencing than our modern farms today.

"And so the cows," he said to me, "could wander round the
	place,
And, since our farms had lots of scrub, were difficult to
	trace."

"To make the job of finding cows a somewhat easier chore,
We'd tie a bell around the neck of, maybe, three or four.
So when we had to round them up in dawn's uncertain grey,
We'd hear the home-made tinkling bells from quite a stretch
	away."

After listening to his story, I gave him my reply;
And I'm glad that Harold noticed the twinkle in my eye.
"I thought they wore a bell," I said, and with a knowing smirk;
"I thought they wore a bell because their horns would never
	work!"

NOT FOR ME!

*(Farming has more than its fair share of accidents, and I, for
one, am glad I'm still in one piece!)*

There's more than a few of my farming mates have lost a
	finger or two
Through doing the jobs all around the farm, and the same
	could happen to you!
The loss of toes or a number of teeth on the farm are not
	unknown,
And many accidents there be that result in a broken bone!
But I reckon I'd give the game away - I'd be tempted to retire,
If I, like a couple of blokes I know, lost an eye when straining
	wire!

FENCING WIRE

I had a roll of fencing wire not all that long ago
Left over from the paddock fence that skirts the flats below.
I don't know where it's got to - I needed some just now,
But the roll is non-existent, it's disappeared somehow.
I know I used a little putting catches on the gates,
And a bit I used for handles on some empty wooden crates.
My kids were going camping, so I made some toasting forks
They could use for cooking damper after long, exhausting
      walks.
I used some in the gardens to help the peas and beans,
But I didn't use a lot of it, no, not by any means!
I put a length across the yard to make the dog a run,
But restrictions, he's decided, are no good to anyone!
The chimney flue was leaning, so I tied it up with wire,
No use using baler twine, for that would catch on fire!
My wife likes hanging baskets, so I made a lot of hooks,
And I used a bit repairing the shed we use for chooks.
But where the roll has got to I haven't got a clue,
And I really need some wire for the job I've got to do.
I know I used some lately on the windmill by the shed,
And I made a small enclosure where the calves are being fed.
Just last week, I reckon, I used some up the track
On a stay that needed mending, it had just begun to crack.
The orchard's being raided, so I fixed the possum trap,
And I used some on the pigsty so the iron wouldn't flap.
It was only just last Tuesday, before I went to town,
That I used some on the woodshed to stop it falling down.
But now the roll has vanished, and so I make this plea,
"Please tell me where it's got to - for I don't know where it
      be!"

EQUINOCTIAL GALES

(There are some disadvantages living on the side of a hill -and this is one of them.)

Some people think Spring's the best time of the year,
But that's not the thought of some folk around here;
For in late September there comes without fail,
A rip-roaring, wild equinoctial gale!

I take our dog walking each day round our block;
It's usually evening - about five o'clock.
But, come late September, she often turns tail;
She hates being out in equinoctial gales!

There's some neighbours of ours who all like to spend
Some time on their yachts almost every weekend.
But, come late September, they haul in their sails,
Admitting defeat to equinoctial gales.

Our house has been built on the side of a hill,
The roof is of iron and remains with us still;
And to keep it secure we doubled the nails,
To ensure it withstands equinoctial gales!

I do like the Spring with its sunshine and showers,
And the courting of birds and the blooming of flowers;
But not late September with all it entails!
I really can't stand equinoctial gales!

A WARM BED

(I never have liked electric blankets, but this was something different! - and better!)

To sit beside the fire at night
When I was young, was pure delight;
I'd watch the flames before I went to bed.
And, through their changing shapes, I'd see
All sorts of things in front of me -
I'd make up wondrous stories in my head.

And, as I dreamed, my Dad would pick
From near the fire, a heated brick,
And carefully wrap it up inside a towel.
My mother, then, at half-past eight,
Would say to us, "It's getting late;
Pick up your things, it's time for bed right now!"

Reluctantly we'd leave the fire,
Off to our bedrooms we'd retire;
We'd slide between the sheets both cold and white.
But Dad had earlier been around,
So we, in winter, always found
A towel-wrapped brick inside our bed each night.

In modern times, as you all know,
Electric blankets are the go,
Just turn a switch and you've got instant heat!
But they don't give to us at all
The bliss we felt when we were small
Of having towel-wrapped bricks warm frozen feet!

THE MANUAL EXCHANGE

('The Manual Telephone Exchange' is now a thing of the past. But, in times gone by, most, if not all telephone calls were connected manually. To telephone anyone, you needed to ring the local exchange, give the number you wished to call, and trusted that the operator would make your connection.
The Manual Exchange was certainly in operation when I first went teaching in the bush. However, some difficulties were encountered, as this poem well illustrates!)

When we headed for the country we found it rather strange
To find we were dependent on a manual exchange.

The telephone, old-fashioned, was screwed upon the wall,
And difficult to manage if you happened to be small.

We'd wind the handle quickly, then patiently would wait
For John or Marj to answer, or, perhaps, their daughter Kate.

Most times they'd answer promptly, and put the number
        through;
But, if they didn't answer, there was nothing you could do.

Thursday night, I think it was, was not a time to call,
For often it was difficult to get put through at all!

You'd give the number wanted, but Marj or John would say
That, "The number you are calling I'm afraid's engaged today."

And, when people tried to ring us, it happened in reverse,
"The Rush's are not answering," she'd say in manner terse.

It wasn't until later that we found why this was so,
Thursday night was card night - but we weren't in the know!

Others in the district, when we happened to complain,
Said, "Auntie Marj's card nights have started up again."

"And anyway," some others said, "What's so wrong with that?
There's still six other evenings if you want to have a chat!"

If you had some private business, or some secrets for a friend,
You wouldn't use the telephone your messages to send!

Marj said they never listened when we spoke upon the 'phone,
But our confidential chatter was quickly widely known.

The system had its drawbacks and was subject to abuse,
But there was the odd occasion that it had a better use.

You could always leave a message for the neighbours round
    about,
And Marj could always tell you who was in and who was out!

Now I know we get nostalgic as the years go on and on,
But the manual telephone exchange I'm glad is dead and gone!

THE SCHOOL CONCERT

(A long-held tradition for many years in the small rural schools throughout our land was the end-of-year concert. Now that the majority of these little schools have been closed, the annual school concert is all but gone in many of our rural communities. The end-of-year concert was one of the community highlights of the year, and, in many districts, almost the entire population would come along, for it was a great social event.

It may have been looked forward to by the local populace, but to the schoolteacher, particularly of the one-teacher school, it was the source of a great deal of work.

Practices, costumes, lines and songs to learn, and the normal school timetable to follow made the final few weeks of the year a bit of a headache to the young teacher, but he, or she, usually came up with the goods, as did the children who also worked hard to see the concert was "as good as last year."

Mind you, the Mothers' Club was also hard at work, and often helped with the costumes, sets, etc. as well as seeing that the supper was, as always, a wonderful spread!

Christmas carols, Christmas plays,
Scones on plates, and cups on trays.
Spotless clothes and neat-brushed hair,
Squalling babes, and squeaking chair.
Stuttered lines, and ill-played notes,
Voices lost in nervous throats.

Dances, skits, and solos, too,
Some done well, some muddled through.
Grandpas, grandmas, dads and mums,
Almost everybody comes.
Raucous laughter, loud applause,
More than one embarrassed pause.
Speeches, thank yous, presentations;
Then a final hesitation
Before the firetruck, siren blaring,
Comes, and all the children, staring,
Cheer as Santa waves his hand,
And smiles from his exalted stand.
As he clambers from the truck,
All the children run amok.
In summer heat, and frantic noise,
He gives to all the gifts and toys.
Supper's next; then plate and cup
Are gathered for the washing up.
Children yawning, rubbing eyes,
Sounds of tired babies' cries.
Cars are started, drive away;
Teacher's thankful that the day
Has passed. He shuts the door,
And tests to see it's locked for sure.
The tension lines have left his face,
But then a hint, the slightest trace
Of more anticipated pain -
Next year the concert's on again!

THE WHITENIN' HOLE

(One of my jobs when I was a youngster was to paint the fireplace with red ochre every Saturday. When I mentioned this to some 'oldies' in my district, they all replied that their fireplaces were always treated daily, and not with red ochre, but with white pipe clay from the local 'whitenin' or whiting hole'.
This method of treating the fireplace was not only widespread in Tasmania, but was also the preferred way of looking after the fireplace in quite a few places in mainland Australia.
What did you do to your fireplace and hearth?)

The whitenin' hole! The whitenin' hole!
Have you all heard of the whitenin' hole?
The folk round here recall it well,
And I, my friends, will attempt to tell
What I have learnt in the last few days
Of our pioneers' ingenious ways.
And, as I do, I'll the praise extol
Of the now out-moded whitenin' hole!

When I was young my mum would ask
If I'd forgotten my weekend task.
"You know you have to paint," she'd say,
"The fireplace bricks each Saturday."
I'd get the brush, and the ochre red,
And mix it up in the garden shed.
Then into the house, and I'd paint with care
The bricks inside each fireplace there.

But things were somewhat different here
In the bygone days of yesteryear.
The fireplace bricks were a lovely sight,
For they weren't red, but a brilliant white.
They'd coat the bricks almost every day
With a single layer of the whitest clay.
Not a sign remained of the blackened coal,
And they got their clay from a whitenin' hole!

If a big tree fell, they would sometimes find
That a largish hole was left behind
Where once the roots and the stump had been,
That was filled with clay so pure and clean
It was used for pipes, and for whitening, too,
The fireplace bricks so they looked like new!
With a dampened rag they would smear the clay
On the blackened firebricks every day!

And where could a whitenin' hole be found?
In a patch of scrub, or on open ground,
On a local farm, or a hillside bare,
A whitenin' hole could be anywhere!
But all the folk around would know
Of the whitenin' hole, and along they'd go
When they needed more - they'd take a tin
Or a whitenin' billy to collect it in.

A whitenin' hole, I've heard folks say,
Could last for years - to this very day
They could show me spots where I could see
Where whitenin' holes once used to be.
Most fires today are seen through glass,
There's few that burn on an open hearth.
So now I know not a single soul
Who gathers clay from a whitenin' hole!

WHAT HAPPENED TO WINTER?

The dawn is breaking early and the hills are turning gold;
I hear the cuckoos calling all day long.
The gentle breezes blowing all have lost their bitter cold,
And the robins and the wrens are full of song.

I heard the bleak predictions of the prophets back in May
Forewarning us that winter would be tough.
"We know there'll be rough weather by the signs we see each
    day;
We'll have a dreadful winter, sure enough!"

But now it is September, and our winter's hurried past,
And very mild and short it proved to be.
We've had no heavy snowstorms, and no Antarctic blast,
The prophets got it wrong, it seems to me.

I met one of them lately, and I gently said, "Hey, Jim!
I thought you said our winter would be long?"
"It was El Nino," he retorted, "But summer will be grim,
And rarely do you find my forecasts wrong!"

THE OLD BLOKE

He's crotchety, cranky, and deaf as a post;
And his manners, when eating, are far worse than most:
Whether biscuits or cake or a slice of cold ham,
Or a piping hot serving of peas and roast lamb,
He gulps all his food with his mouth open wide.
We often feel tempted to put him outside
To eat all his meals - but he's now very old,
We feel he would suffer too much in the cold.
He's lost all his teeth, his hair has turned white,
He's not what you'd call the handsomest sight!
He growls at the children, he's rude to our friends,
He snores through the telly, and wakes when it ends.
It isn't old Grandpa I'm talking about,
It's our ageing old dog, and it's time he went out!

WATER-CARTING SEASON

(A perennial complaint of those who rely on tankwater!)

"Do you have to take an hour
Every time you take a shower?"
I ask my city daughters when they come across to stay.
"And do you think that, maybe,
Each time you bath the baby,
That the bath's not filled completely, but just a little way?"

The dams are getting lower,
And the creek runs ever slower,
But my visitors use water at a quite alarming rate.
And I say to them politely,
"Don't use our water lightly;
We're all on tanks, remember, and it's pretty dry of late."

"When hands or teeth you're brushing,
Don't leave the water rushing,
Just use a little water, or it'll soon be gone."
But, regardless of my pleading
On how much we are needing
To be careful with the water, the taps run on and on.

Now it's water-carting season,
And I'm sure you know the reason
Why I'm busy carting water and my tanks are nearly dry.
For my visitors and daughters
Have used up all our water,
And, without a pang of conscience, they've left and waved
        good-bye!

OLD MACDONALD (with apologies!)

(Just a bit of fun! - But, maybe, with more than an ounce or two of truth!)

Old Macdonald had a farm, but now he's walking out;
For his property's gone bust through seven years of drought!

Old Macdonald had a farm, a biggish one he chose,
But now he's off - the bank has said it's going to foreclose.

Old Macdonald had a farm, but had to leave it when
The price of beef and price of wool went through the floor
      again!

Old Macdonald had a farm, but now it has been sold,
The family wouldn't take it on, and he is growing old.

Old Macdonald had a farm, but now it can't be used,
So much spraying has been done it's chemically abused!

Old Macdonald had a farm, but now he's going bust,
The crop he grows has now succumbed to some resistant rust!

Old Macdonald had a farm, and things were due to boom,
But all his dams and waterways have got an algal bloom!

Old Macdonald had his farm, he's had it up to here!
He's going to sell it and retire later in the year!

THE RASPBERRY PICKER

(Another poem inspired by Auntie Kath! Although her days of raspberry picking are now well past, she remembers enthusiastically how she enjoyed gathering the harvest!

She did tell me about a young fellow who tried to beat her at picking raspberries. Apparently he came straight from a late night dance at the local Hall and started picking raspberries before sun-up!

"I still beat him by the end of the day!" she told me, with a grin!)

She was a raspberry picker once, and few could do it better,
She'd pick them morning, noon, and night if folks had only let
    her!
There was a plot upon their farm that grew the sweetest crop,
And, when the harvesting was on, she didn't want to stop!

She'd put her picking pocket on - a tin it was, with ties,
She'd put it on around her waist - 'twas just the proper size!
She'd pick the raspberries fast and clean, and, when she filled
    the tin,
She'd go to where her bucket was, and tip the raspberries in.

The buckets, there were lots of them, were very much home
    made,
And painted on each bucket was a number, well displayed;
For every raspberry picker had a number handed out,
So the boss could tell exactly who picked what, without a
    doubt.

These buckets were a squarish shape, they'd all held kerosene,
Four gallons each I think they held, and had a silver sheen.

The top of each had been cut out, and handles made of wire,
And cheap, efficient pails they were, and easy to acquire.

The pickers always had a race to see who picked the best,
But Auntie Kath, for she it was, she usually beat the rest!
At times she picked, or so I'm told, two hundred pounds a day,
Even though she'd have to spend an hour or two away.

For she would often have to help prepare the pickers' lunch,
And that would take a bit of time, they were a hungry bunch!
But, even then, she beat them, no matter how they tried,
"Few could pick them quicker," she mentions now, with pride.

The buckets would be emptied into barrels made of wood,
With, of course, the farmer checking that all the fruit was
        good!
And then the barrels went to town upon an ancient truck,
Where Jones and Co. would pay a premium price, with any
        luck!

The raspberries were all treated in their big evaporator,
And stored until the factory hands, a little while later,
Made the raspberries into jam, and, as far as I can tell,
The jam was tinned or bottled and then labelled "IXL".

But that was many years ago, it doesn't happen now,
The plot of canes has long since gone, but Kath still tells me
        how
In years long past she'd have a race with every raspberry
        picker,
And few there were that beat her, for she'd always pick them
        quicker.

WEIGHTY PROBLEMS

(The first time the last poem "The Raspberry Picker" was broadcast on radio, I had a telephone call from an retired employee of one of the companies who bought raspberries from the local farmers.
The raspberries that were brought to the factory were in water and, although most of the farmers were scrupulously honest, there were a few who would add extra water, or even rocks, to increase the weight of the raspberries.
This retired 'berryman' told me this story, and insisted it was absolutely true!)

A factory had a berryman, I don't recall his name,
And he it was who had to check the raspberries that came
From farms throughout the district - the farmers brought them
    in,
Using casks of wood, or buckets, or silver-sided tins.

The tins had once held kerosene, and were an ideal size
For carting raspberries to and fro, and also to disguise
The true amount of berries; for all were stored in water,
And occasionally these tins contained more water than they
    oughta!

36

This, of course, increased the weight, and hence the buyer's
    cost,
And also it was not unknown that sometimes rocks were
    tossed
Into the berry tins as well to add a pound or two,
But, to be fair, most farmers were honest through and through.

But those who weren't were problems, the berryman could tell
The ones who tried to hoodwink, and he, of course, knew well
That sometimes girls or boys were hired to use a can or cup
To add water to the silver tins just to top them up!

One farmer in the district, a Mr. Bloggs by name,
Was famous for this practice, and one day when he came
To sell his daily harvest, he was given a demand
To come and see the berryman, who gave this reprimand.

"Your raspberries weigh heavier than others that come in;
Now we cope with rocks in buckets, we cope with sloppy tins.
But, with the extra water, would you please, dear Mr. Bloggs,
Tell your boy to strain it carefully, for we cannot cope with
    frogs!"

SIGNS OF WEATHER

(Weather forecasters cop a lot of flak, but, if the truth be known, we all like to think we can do a bit of forecasting ourselves!
There's many who say they can predict what the weather will be, short or long-term, by various natural signs - how about you?)

Scurrying ants and mackerel sky,
Galloping horses racing by;
Aching joints, black cockatoos,
There's any number we can choose
Of natural signs to help us know
What rains will fall, what winds will blow.
The cat may wash behind his ear,
The moon may look a trifle queer;
The seagulls flock, or chimneys smoke,
Or myriad little frogs may croak.
From simple signs we ascertain
A winter cold, or flooding rain.
The way the chooks peck in the yard,
Or kookaburras laughing hard:
A possum's coat, a roaring sea,
A cricket's chirp, a buzzing bee,
Are all, at times, a weather sign
Predicting rain, or hail, or shine.
But I've been told, without a doubt,
That all signs fail in times of drought!!!

DROUGHT 1998

(The nineteen nineties have seen great swathes of our country suffer some of the most devastating droughts in our short history. Nineteen ninety-eight was no exception, and I am continually amazed at the resilience and optimism of so many of our suffering farmers and graziers.)

Paddocks bare, and hungry stock,
Dams are dry and hard as rock.
Tanks are low, and rivers, too,
Flow has stopped in quite a few.
The creek is now a bed of dust,
It's hard for farms to make a crust.
Money's tight, and times are tough;
Some rain's come, but not enough.
Hay is dear and hard to get,
And the drought's not over yet.
It's hard to see how some will cope,
But farmers have amazing hope.
For hope in farmers springs eternal,
And most will beat this drought infernal!!

THE COUNTRY HOSPITAL

(The past few years have seen the demise of many of the local institutions that were once considered sacrosanct. Many of the small rural schools have been closed, and banks have been closing their country branches at an enormous rate. Many Government services seem to be have been reduced, or removed altogether from our small communities and towns.

The local country hospital has also suffered, and many have now been closed, and a lot of rural folk have found that they now need to travel long distances if they need the services that only a hospital can offer.

I, for one, do not agree with all these closures, and it is difficult not to have the opinion that, in some ways, country people are treated as second-class citizens by the powers that be!

Hence this poem!)

Our little country hospitals are closing one by one,
No matter how efficient, it seems their days are done;
Authorities, if you ask me, consider only size,
And so you hear them argue that it's best to centralise.

A little country hospital was where our girl was born;
The first of four fair daughters, she came at early dawn.
This little country hospital was on the edge of town,
And, looking from the window, there were paddocks all
      around.

My wife, with baby daughter, would watch this peaceful scene,
No views of concrete canyons, just lovely pastures green.
And early every morning to welcome in the day,
A cow and calf beyond the fence not thirty yards away.

This little country hospital was used throughout the years
For many operations, and saw its share of tears.
But lives of many folk were saved, and it was always there,
A symbol of community, a sign of love and care.

Heart attacks and broken limbs, poisoning and strokes,
Treated by the doctors who were well-known local blokes.
And when there were emergencies, as far as I can tell,
The hospital's proximity helped survival rates as well.

So now our country hospital is going to shut its doors;
And I cannot say for certain that the next one won't be yours!
We didn't want the place to shut, but we don't have a say;
And now our nearest hospital is many miles away.

Why was our little hospital forced to disappear?
Few voters in the country? Or other reason queer?
Or economic rationalism gone absolutely mad?
Whatever is the reason, to us country folk it's sad!

FOR SALE

(These verses may give some indication of what I think about so many of our public bodies and institutions being privatised. I may also have provided an alternative - I wonder if you agree with me?)

"Privatise! We'll privatise!" is all we've heard for years
From Governments around our land, and they receive the
    cheers
Of Corporations, rich and large, and business men of note,
Who say, "If we don't privatise we're sure to miss the boat!"

The banks, both Commonwealth and State, are now in private
    hands,
And our National Airline, too, that flies to other lands
Has long been privatised as well, as have our railways, too;
And the dear old CES has also owners new.

Electric power is privatised in many of our States;
They tell us it is good for us - it's sure to lower rates.
Airports have been leased or sold to those who bid the most;
And Telstra has been partly sold - what next? Australia Post?

The list is growing every year - some say it does us harm
To privatise so many things - "We're selling off the farm!"
But we hear in every State the politicians say
That much we have should now be sold unless each pays its
    way!

So what is in their pipeline now? Our bridges? Roads? Our
    docks?
Or, maybe, all our National Parks - their trees and lakes and
    rocks.
Perhaps our rivers, creeks and dams, and beaches could be
    sold,
So long as Governments can sell these things for wealth
    untold!

But wait a sec! I have a thought on what is best to sell;
Although it mightn't suit some folk, but one can never tell.
Let's privatise our Governments, that sounds a splendid
    mission;
I wonder what's the going rate for Federal politicians?

MEASUREMENT - A CONUNDRUM

(Can you answer this question I pose at the end of the verse?)

Hundredweights and ounces, quarters, stones and grains,
Furlongs, yards and inches, feet and links and chains;
Acres, roods and perches, pennyweights and miles,
Finding crooked sixpences, and climbing crooked stiles.
Bushels, pecks and gallons, pints and gills and quarts,
Shillings, pounds and pennies -that's what I was taught.
No longer do we find them in any school exams,
It's metres now, and hectares, litres, tonnes and grams.
Everything is metric, even drums and kegs -
So why, if all is metric, can we buy a dozen eggs?

FISH AND CHIPS

(A little nostalgia - nothing can beat the fish and chips that were wrapped in newspaper!!)

The tramfare was twopence when I went to school,
The tramfare was twopence, but I, as a rule,
Was driven to school in a massive old car,
Which was, you'd imagine, my preference by far.
But though partly right, on occasions I'd choose
To walk home from school in my black, leather shoes.
I'd walk the five miles, if the weather was fine,
I'd walk the five miles, and the twopence was mine!
Now twopence was twopence, and, during my hike,
I'd stop at the fish-shop and buy what I'd like.
A penn'orth of chips, some potato cakes, too,
All wrapped in "The Herald" as all used to do.
I'd stuff the whole package just under my coat,
And tear off the end, and happily gloat
To all of the kids that I happened to meet
As I feasted my way down the bitumened street.
And, if I was careful, and didn't eat fast,
I found that my flavoursome banquet would last
To the top of the lane that led to the gate
At the back of our house - where I'd arrive late!
I'd walk in the kitchen, and mother would see,
And gently rebuke with "You won't eat your tea!"
But my hunger returned every time without fail.
And now, as I come to the end of my tale,
I'll have to admit there's no chips anywhere
That can match those I bought with my twopenny fare!

MOUNT WELLINGTON

(For all those who live, or have lived in Hobart, Mount Wellington is simply known as 'The Mountain'. It towers over the city, and is a part of life to all Hobartians.)

Once known as Table Mountain, and then Skiddaw, I'm told,
The backdrop to the city is a wonder to behold!
We call it now Mount Wellington, in honour of the name
Of he who won at Waterloo, and earned eternal fame!
It towered above Old Hobart Town, and towers above us yet,
An icon in the broadest sense, a sight one ne'er forgets.
It has a thousand different moods, depending on the weather,
And, when completely lost in fog, it has no mood whatever!
On cloud-bound days it has been known to have a sullen
     frown,
But one can almost see it smile when dawn bedecks its crown!
In winter, dressed in brilliant white, it often seems asleep,
But, when the rain runs down its cheeks, one sees the
     mountain weep.
As storm-clouds gather overhead above its face and back,
The mountain can be threatening, with mood both stern and
     black!
Its mood is drear and most forlorn on cheerless winter days,
But it appears ethereal when viewed through summer haze.
When snow is sprinkled on its crown it has a festive look,
Reminding one of Christmas pud. that mother used to cook!
Through all its ever-changing moods, it towers above us still,
And, as long as Hobart's here, our Mountain always will!

PS. *(My wife Yvonne provided her own final line -*
"The Mountain we call Wellington, a dirty, great big hill!)

LOOKING FOR RAIN

(We are a nation of sky-watchers, always keeping an eye out for any signs of a weather change. I am one of the chief culprits in this regard!)

The day was warm at an early hour,
We could clearly see the Wellington tower.

By nine a.m. the day was hot,
And promised hotter, like as not.

By afternoon it reached forty degrees,
Helped along by the northerly breeze.

Some flimsy clouds were seen up high
At two o'clock in the western sky.

A rounded moon at twilight shone
To show the clouds had passed and gone.

As dusk descended into night
The stars appeared as points of light.

When midnight came I heaved a sigh,
For still we had a cloudless sky.

I won't look overhead again,
A sky that's watched will never rain!

HOW PETER WON
THE CAULFIELD CUP

*(I was 'writer-in-residence' for a weekend in South Gippsland
some years ago, and a delightful weekend it turned out to be!
The whole group travelled in gypsy caravans, each pulled by
a gentle giant of a Clydesdale. One of these horses, Fred, was
a little lazy, so the owner{I'll call him Peter} sometimes
hurried him along with the threat of a cattle prod.
Peter was a very large man, and Fred was a very large
Clydesdale, so they were well matched. I told the group they
would each need to have written something to share around the
campfire on the final night, and this was my contribution.)*

Peter took a gypsy wagon down to Melbourne Town today;
He went to see the Caulfield Cup, but had no place to stay;
So he camped beside the race-track, and he had a bet or two,
And, with each successive wager, his pot of money grew.

His wagon horses he unhitched just prior to the Cup,
And, holding Fred by hairy mane, he tied the other up.
Before he haltered Fred he clambered up onto his back,
And had his private grandstand there beside the racing track.

Now on his wagon Pete had left his vicious cattle prod,
For Fred would sometimes misbehave, he was a lazy sod!
And, as the starter had the field all safely stalled in line,
Fred took a backward step and felt the prod in his behind!

The frightened Fred leapt o'er the fence just as the race began,
And thirty thousand people roared as Fred, with rider, ran
Beside the speeding horses as round the track they raced,
While Peter hung on grimly, embarrassed and red-faced!

Two hundred metres from the line Fred bolted to the lead,
And, though they tried, the others couldn't match the
     Clydesdale's speed.
The judges all decided Fred had won by half a nose,
Which didn't please the jockeys who came very close to
     blows!

The bookies were delighted, but the punters greatly vexed,
For the heavily backed favourite was the horse which came in
     next!
But their anger turned to cheers - the result had been reversed;
The stewards found Pete underweight, and placed the favourite
     first!

MACHINERY

(I am no mechanic! If one of my chainsaws, mowers, pumps, etc., misbehave, I usually have to find someone who can help fix it for me.
Simple problems I can manage, but my machines seem to take a delight in being obtuse by having strange things go wrong with them - and ALWAYS, ALWAYS at a time when I really need to use them!!!)

Why is it, when you need them most,
 Machines we use give up the ghost?
Whipper-snippers, mowers, too,
Chainsaws, whether old or new,
All decide to fade and die
At some untimely moment. Why?

We have a tank up on the hill
Which, regularly, I have to fill
From other tanks, which fill again
Each time we get a decent rain.
The hilltop tank is needed so
The water in our taps will flow.

Of late we had a dryish spell,
And it's not difficult to tell
Our water was a little short.
And then it rained. "Good-o!" I thought,
"I'll pump the water up tonight;
The top tank's sounding pretty light!"

Our pump's a fire-fighting one,
For three years straight it's always run
Reliably, and with a roar:
But this time it was feeling sore;
It coughed and blew a lot of smoke,
And finished with a feeble croak.

I asked it nicely if it could
Behave as all machinery should.
But no! It wouldn't run at all,
Or walk, or skip, or even crawl!
Each time I tried to make it start,
It cried, as of a broken heart!

And, though we've had a lot of rain,
Our water's running short again.
The pump is at the doctor's now,
He thinks it can be cured somehow!
Why is it, when we need them most,
Our machines give up the ghost?

THE OUTBACK

("THE OUTBACK" is a well-known term to all Australians, and each of us has a slightly different understanding of what constitutes 'THE OUTBACK', where are its boundaries, and is it just an area of land somewhere in Australia, or is there something more to it?
This poem is my attempt to try and give some definition to the term "THE OUTBACK". Feel free to disagree with me!!)

The Outback! Where's the Outback? Is it somewhere back of
      Bourke?
Or where the pioneer drovers did their pioneering work?
Is it out beyond the Darling? Or out past Uluru?
Or is it where it never rains, and skies are always blue?

Some find it in the gibber where the summer heat's intense;
Some find it on the treeless plains beyond the Dingo Fence,
Or through the Simpson Desert where the sand is never still,
Where the loneliness and silence can daunt the stoutest will.

I've found it west of Broken Hill, and south of Longreach, too,
Where coolibah and gidyea grow beside the great Barcoo.
I've found it in the Flinders where the creek so rarely run,
Where the mountains are a picture as they watch the setting
      sun.

Now all of these are places, and I'm sure it's true to say
That they all reflect the Outback, and will for many a day.
But the Outback's more than places, more than things to go
      and see,
It's a quality or essence in the heart of you and me.

The Outback features highly in the spirit of our land;
It's more than distant mountains, it's more than drifting sand.
You'll find it in our history, in the lives of many a bloke,
In our swaggies, drovers, stockmen, and the hardy womenfolk.

You cannot grasp the Outback, not completely, anyway,
For its spirit is elusive in a most frustrating way.
You can sense the Outback's presence, you can know that's
        where you are,
Whether in the streets of Melbourne, or east of Marble Bar.

You can journey to the Outback in an actual literal sense,
Smell the scent of desert breezes, touch the ancient Dingo
        Fence:
But that isn't what the Outback ever was, or isn't now,
It is in part, for certain, but it's more than that, somehow.

The intangible component, the very heart and soul
Is needed to be present to make the Outback whole.
And the spirit of the Outback can be partly felt and heard
In the writings of our poets as they share the written word.

The Outback isn't only in the great beyond "out there",
For the spirit of the Outback is for all of us to share.
It pulses through our history with a never-ending beat,
From the Ranges west of Alice to the cold, suburban street.

When the situation's trying and the circumstances tough;
When life is full of problems and the going's looking rough,
We see the Outback surface in a man's laconic grin,
In the psyche of the battler who refuses to give in.

The Outback is the mettle, it's the steel within us all,
We feel it's distant drumbeat, and we hear its tireless call.
There is an actual Outback, but it's only seen in part,
For the spirit of the Outback is within the nation's heart!

DROP DUST HERE!

(As I was driving through outback Queensland a year or two ago, I noticed an odd sign beside the road. The sign said "DROP DUST HERE!"
It so intrigued me that I wrote this poem.)

"DROP DUST HERE!" the notice said,
In painted letters large and red.
"DROP DUST HERE!" The car I slowed
To read this sign beside the road.
"DROP DUST HERE! Was this a joke
Played by quirky outback folk?
All I could see for miles around
Was dusty road and dusty ground!
I'd driven west from Isis Downs
Towards a little outback town,
When, just before the great Barcoo,
This sign instructs me what to do!
"DROP DUST HERE!" I wish I could;
The car is dust from wheels to hood!
But no way could I make it drop,
And so I didn't even stop!
I just deliberately ignored
That painted sign - and, rest assured,
That, though I chose to disobey,
No twinge of guilt I felt that day!

WAITING!

(I am frequently asked when and where I write my poems, and from where do I get my ideas. The answer to this is that I carry a notebook and pencil wherever I go, and write while sitting having a coffee in a restaurant, waiting at the doctor's, or the airport, or wherever I may be. I also jot down any ideas that might come to mind, whether from a conversation I'm having, something I see, or, maybe, even a news item or something I see on television.

This poem I started writing when I was listening to music being played over the telephone, after some recorded message had told me how valued my custom was, and someone would attend to me shortly!!

Oh! By the way! I nearly finished the poem before I was spoken to by a real live person on the other end of the telephone!)

Waiting!
We do it when we're standing up and when we're sitting
      down;
We do it in our fancy clothes and in our dressing gown;
We do it with a pleasant smile and do it with a frown,
We do it in the country and we do it in the town -
It's waiting!

Waiting!
We sit and wait while answer-phones speak out their little
      spiel;
We sit and wait in restaurants for lunch or evening meal.
When playing cards we sit and wait for somebody to deal,
And no one seems to care about the impatience we can feel
When waiting!

Waiting!
We stand and wait at traffic lights, we wait to cross the street;
We stand and wait for bus or train on tired and aching feet.
We stand and wait to buy our food, our groceries and meat.
Outside the gates of sporting grounds in rain and wind and
      heat,
We're waiting!

Waiting!
We wait at airports for our friends who come from towns
      remote,
We sometimes wait for those to leave on ferry, yacht, or boat.
At election times, of course, we wait to cast our vote,
And, afterwards, we wait to hear the politicians gloat:
We're waiting!

Waiting!
We wait in line to buy our stamps when mail we wish to send:
We stand and wait in shops and stores as wc our money
      spend.
The hours that we waste waiting could send us round the
      bend!
And now you're sitting quietly and hope this poem will end!
You're waiting!

THE THYLACINE

(The Thylacine, also known as the Tasmanian Tiger or Tasmanian Wolf, has been presumed extinct in the wild for now well over sixty years. The last captive Thylacine died in the Hobart Zoo in 1933.
Persistent reports of sightings in a number of areas in Tasmania, however, keep alive a faint glimmer of hope that the Thylacine has managed to avoid extinction.
The most recent report was as late as January 1999, and the sighting was certainly not dismissed out of hand. So, who knows, the Thylacine may still exist, but, until hard evidence is forthcoming, we won't know for certain.
The Hobart Museum had a "Thylacine Exhibition" in 1998, and I wrote this poem for a radio programme that was highlighting this particular exhibition.)

Thylacine! O Thylacine!
There's few are left have ever seen
A living, breathing Thylacine!

Thylacine, O Thylacine!
It seems there was no in-between,
'Twas all or none for Thylacine!

Tasmanian Tiger - just a pest,
Our ancestors were not distressed
When to extinction you were pressed.

Tasmanian Tiger, gone for good;
We blame our fathers - I wonder would
We have saved you if we could?

Tasmanian Wolf with loping gait,
Settlers came and sealed your fate;
We want you now - but all too late!

Tasmanian Wolf, your life has flown;
We have some skin and whitened bone,
And remnants in some fossilled stone.

Australians all, why can't we see
That be it bird, or beast, or tree,
We, too, can as destructive be!

IF FARMERS WENT ON STRIKE

(Our nation has had its share of strikes. We've had shearers'
strikes, wharfies' strikes, teachers' strikes, nurses' strikes, air-
pilots' strikes, and even a police strike!
All of these strikes cause some disruption to our normal
lifestyle, some more so than others.
But have you ever thought what would happen if other sectors
of our society went on strike? If mothers, for example, decided
to go on strike, there would be pandemonium! There are
some who would say that, if politicians went on strike, probably
no-one would notice!
But, if farmers went on strike, it would not be long before all
members of our society felt the effects, and very severe they
would be, indeed!)

The wharfies and the shearers, the trains' and buses' crew,
Have all been out on strike at times, and, maybe, so have you.
The teachers and the nurses, they've had their turns as well,
And they caused a few disruptions, as far as I could tell.
But have you ever wondered what the chaos would be like
If all our nation's farmers decided they would strike?

We'd have no milk for breakfast, for coffee or for tea,
And I know how that would trouble the likes of even me!
I always have my porridge, I have it every day,
With milk and maple syrup; imagine my dismay,
And all the other households, if milk could not be bought,
I reckon half the nation would start off out of sorts.

There'd be no steaks or rissoles, no sausages or chops,
So people's socialising would, very largely, stop.
Australians love to party, and barbecues are best,
But, without a steak or sausage, the barbie's laid to rest!
And Australia's social fabric would show a lot of cracks
If the workforce of our nation was unable to relax!

How much our health would suffer is difficult to tell
If all our market gardeners joined in the strike as well.
And, if the strike was lengthy, not over in a week,
It's scary to imagine what havoc it would wreak!
Just think of all the products that originate on farms,
The shortage of these items would cause us much alarm!

No leather goods or flour, and hence no shoes or bread,
No hops, and hence no beer - the thought fills some with
          dread!
No wool or cotton either, no comfy socks or coats,
And I would have no porridge if I couldn't get some oats!
I could go on for ever, but I think you've got my gist,
If we had striking farmers, they'd be very greatly missed!

THE BOOBOOK OWL

The night was clear,
The air was still,
And I could hear
The insects shrill.

But then a call,
"Morepork," I heard.
In gum tree tall
I saw the bird.

Against the moon
A Boobook round,
Its two-note tune
My favourite sound.

I went inside
For it was late.
I lay beside
My sleeping mate.

I listened long;
The owl again
Continued on
Its sweet refrain.

To gently fall
Asleep at night,
As Boobooks call
Is sheer delight!

TUSSOCK BROOMS

(As I visit different places, I find it most interesting to hear about local customs, and, in the case of the older generation, how things were in their younger days.

Often I find that there was much in common in people's lives many years ago, even if they lived in communities many hundreds of miles apart. Home-made Coolgardie Safes, using pipe-clay to paint firebricks, and, as written in this poem, making brooms from tussocks.

My first lesson on how to make a tussock broom was by someone in the Huon Valley in southern Tasmania. A little later I received my second lesson; this time from an eighty-year old fellow I met at Bega, in New South Wales. Both lessons were most informative, and I pass them on to you!)

"I need a new broom," my grandmother said.
"I need a new broom for the yard and the shed."
My grandfather nodded, then slowly replied,
"I'll make one this morning when I go outside."

These words you'll not hear in a farmhouse today,
For Granny's long gone - now I'm going grey!
But, back in the twenties, and even before,
Many brooms in the country weren't bought at a store.

They were made by the farmer or, maybe, his spouse,
As was much of the gear that was used round the house.
The curtains, the aprons, the rugs on the floor,
The shutters, the shingles, the steps at the door.

So off to the paddock my grandfather went;
A considerable time there the old fellow spent,

Looking for just the right tussock to chose
To make into a broom for my Grandma to use.

How did he choose one? Well, I'll tell you how;
He'd sit and he'd watch a bullock or cow
Come up to a tussock and tug on the grass,
And, if it broke easily, that tussock he'd pass.

But, if the cow pulled, and the stem didn't break,
Then Grandpa would think, "Maybe this one I'll take."
But he knew, for certain, the best one to find
Was, when the grass broke, she fell on her behind!

He took out his axe when this tussock he found,
And chopped it right off very close to the ground:
A handle he made from a sapling nearby,
Then back to the house to give it a try.

He poked up the stick where the tussock was cut,
And bound twine very tightly to tie on the butt.
Once the tussock was tied on the handle, he then
Bent the grass blades all double and bound them again.

Then all that my grandfather needed to do
To give to my grandma a broom spanking new,
Was to trim it all neatly - an axe did the job,
And, hey presto! a broom for the yard, shed and hob.

But not any more, those old days are past
When Grandpa made brooms that were tough and would last
For a couple of years; he made them himself,
But we don't do that, we buy off the shelf!

BOOTS

(Boots seem to last and last and last - and mine are no exception.)

My boots are made of leather,
And are fit for any weather,
Be it snow or pouring rain or summer heat.
I've been wearing them for ever
And, I tell you, they have never
Been anything but comfy on my feet.

I haven't cleaned them often,
Although it's meant to soften
The leather, and slow down the wear and tear.
There's two or three deep gashes
From some rather careless slashes
Of the trusty axe I carry everywhere.

They look a little battered,
Not that that has mattered,
And the elastic sides are starting now to fray.
The soles are black and toughened,
The uppers scuffed and roughened,
But I'm sure they'll last for ever and a day.

FOOTBALL

(I love sport!
Mind you, I'm not alone in that, for we are a nation of sport-
lovers. Cricket, swimming, surfing, Australian Rules Football,
Rugby Union, Rugby League, horse-racing, golf, bowls,
basketball, - the list goes on and on!
My love of sport started at a very early age, and I have spent
many of my rather large number of years being an active
participant in one sport or another.
In rural Australia, there is a strong tradition of sport
participation, and it is common to see, both in the heat of summer
and the freezing depths of winter, the local young people - and
not so young - out practising, preparing for their next encounter
with the enemy - another rural community's team!
Some would say 'You have to be mad to play football' - here is
my response to that statement.)

"You have to be mad to play football, a little bit soft in the
        head;
You have to be mad to play football." That's what some
        psychiatrist said.
But I, who played footy often, although many seasons ago,
Would dispute this specialist's statement, and say that this isn't
        so.

Let me start talking of training, two hours two nights of the
    week,
In the deep Victorian winter, the weather both bitter and bleak.
What better activities are there than running around in the dark
Obeying the coach's instructions, the one with the sar-major's
    bark?

I could be home watching the telly, or reading a book by the
    fire;
But exercise surely is better, it's good for the heart to perspire.
When I caught the 'flu or bronchitis, or a nasty cold in the
    head,
It kept my immune system working, not lying round dormant
    instead!

"You have to be mad to play football." That's a pretty rash
    statement to make;
What else can one do at the weekend, how else can one take
    a break?
After working from Monday to Friday, a bloke needs to wind
    down a bit,
And playing two hours of footy helps keep our younger chaps
    fit.

A game on a Saturday arvo, that's what everyone needs;
I guess a few bones may be broken, some noses and cuts
    suffer bleeds.
Oh! we may have a stoush in the middle, there may be a black
    eye or two,
But working at home in the garden can give you an injury,
    too.

I played many seasons of football, and both of my knees are
    intact;
Neither my legs have been broken, although one was partially
    cracked.
Although I sprained both of my ankles, today they are working
    just fine;
My mates have lost teeth by the mouthful, but the teeth in my
    head are all mine.

I've not had a knee reconstruction, 'though most of my mates
    have had two.
My shoulder still plagues me a little, and my neck sometimes
    bothers me, too.
But what's a few cuts and abrasions, an injury or two here and
    there?
It's not only 'cause I played football, it's normal, I say, wear
    and tear.

"You have to be mad to play football!" What else is a fella to
    do?
When he's young and he's fairly athletic, and a little high-
    spirited, too?
We all need a good rough-and-tumble, and better it's done in
    a game,
Than in the back streets of a city between gangs with
    despicable names.

When so many work in an office, a shop, or the factory-room
    floor,
What better to do at the weekend than a game that is played
    out-of-door?
Who wants to be by the fireside, or watching a film or a play?
Regardless of Saturday's weather, fresh air is best any day.

I've played footy up in the mountains, in the wind and the cold
    and the sleet;
I've played in a Wimmera dust-storm, in over the century heat.
I've played on a ground under water, I've played on the side of
    a hill,
And, if my body would let me, I'd be off playing Aussie Rules
    still.

"You have to be mad to play football!" I guess I'm as sane as
    the rest;
But I played many seasons of footy, and I gave it my all and
    my best.
"You have to be mad to play football!" If that statement is
    true,
I'd rather be labelled a crackpot than not to play footy –
    wouldn't you?

BUSHWALKING - AGAIN!

(I've hiked and bushwalked all my life - and loved it!
Nowadays, however, the head and heart are more willing than
the body! But when one shifts to Tasmania to live, the call of the
mountains, the bush, and the beach is powerful, so it's difficult
not to go 'a-wanderin'!
Unfortunately, my body - and that of my mate's - no longer like
carrying the loads they once managed with ease; bushwalking
becomes harder with age!
This poem tells of one recent four-day expedition into the
mountains of Tasmania's South-West.)

We've done it again,
Us two ageing men,
We've staggered off into the hills.
With forty-pound packs,
And broken-down backs,
You'd think we're a couple of dills!

Young Rob came along,
He's both fit and strong,
And still in his forties, I'd say.
When he strides on ahead
He leaves us for dead!
We're plodders, not walkers, today.

We start off at dawn,
Us blokes, old and worn,
We need all the light we can get.

Our travel is slow
As upward we go,
And there's miles still ahead of us yet!

It comes into rain,
So we rest once again,
Our wet-weather gear's what we need.
We put it all on,
Then it's up and we're gone;
Our bodies are weary indeed!

At last! Here's the top!
Once more we can stop
And have ourselves something to eat.
But we're only halfway,
And it's late in the day,
So it's soon that we're back on our feet.

The down-track is steep,
So we warily creep
As we sigh and we puff and we blow.
We slide and we slip,
We stumble and trip,
As we head for the campsite below.

We all give a shout
As the track levels out,
But our cheer's premature, I'm afraid.
Mud up to our thighs,
Scrub whipping our eyes,
No wonder I'm feeling dismayed!

I'm nearly done in,
But I manage a grin
As we come to the end of our walk.
We set up our camp
In the mist and the damp,
But I'm really too weary to talk!

....

But my spirits are buoyed
By the days we enjoyed
That followed our wearisome trek.
But time passes, so then
We walk homeward again;
I fear for my shoulders and neck!

But they somehow survive;
I arrive home alive,
Though I'm stiff from my head to my toes.
I soak in a bath
For an hour and a half,
And my stiffness and weariness goes.

But still my bones creak
For nearly a week,
And my back has its quota of pain.
Yet I'll have to admit
That, once I am fit,
I'll be walking the bush once again!

GENEALOGY

*(I had been asked to speak at a Genealogical Society Dinner,
and so prepared this 'tongue-in-cheek' poem.
Parts of it are true, my mother's maiden name was Lacey, and
my great-great-great grandfather was shipwrecked on the
'Rockingham' in 1829.
What is true, and what is fiction? I'll let you work that one out!)*

My great-great-great grandfather, in eighteen twenty-eight,
Had had enough of England, so he chose to emigrate.
He brought his family with him, but oh! Alack-a-day!
The "Rockingham" he sailed on was wrecked along the way!

Just south of Perth it happened, in eighteen twenty-nine,
But they were all survivors, these ancestors of mine!
The ship hit rocks and foundered some distance from the
    shore,
'Twas Uncle Bob who told me -I'd not heard the tale before.

"Twas Uncle Bob who told me, but that's not all he said;
I wish I'd listened carefully, for now my uncle's dead.
But, on my final visit, my uncle gave to me
A sheet with writing on it, a detailed family tree.

I studied it with interest, I read it through and through,
I found it most enlightening, but maybe not to you!
My great-grandma was Irish, I've cousins in Tyrone,
I guess that's why my mother said I'd kissed the Blarney-stone!

As I studied every name upon the family tree,
I managed to recall some words that Bob had said to me.
"Our ancestor," my Uncle said, "that's on your mother's side,
Came with the Norman Conquest on a strongly-flowing tide."

I thought about this quite a bit, and then I read some more,
But, as the morning passed away, my eyes got really sore.
I shut them then for half a tick, just to take a rest;
And soon I felt my heavy head go nodding to my chest.

I slept through half the afternoon, and had some dreams, as
        well,
And some of them, perhaps, are true, it's difficult to tell.
I can still remember them, I'll one to you relate,
And if it's fact or fiction is for you to arbitrate!

It was the year ten sixty-six when William came from France:
He conquered Harold and the rest, they didn't stand a chance!
A Count de Lacy came with him, and fought by William's
        side;
And, when they'd won, he settled down, and took an English
        bride.

As the centuries came and went, the family tree increased,
And, by the eighteen hundreds, ten thousand folk, at least
Were living in the British Isles who each could say, with
        pride,
They were descended from the Count who fought by William's
        side.

Now one of these descendants was my great-aunt's Uncle Bill,
And he was second cousin to a certain Thomas Hill.
Now Thomas's great-uncle was the Earl of Sodden Vale,
Who was, sadly, killed in battle on the fields of Armadale.

But the Earl's great-grandpa Harry had an older brother, Jim,
And a younger brother, Stewart, but nothing's known of him.
But Jim's great-uncle Noah, in sixteen twenty-four,
Took a trip across to Calais, and was shipwrecked on the
      shore.

Now we have a family motto "Nothing Ventured, Nothing
      Gained."
So Noah walked to Paris where he married, and remained.
And Louis, who was King of France, found place for him in
      court,
So Noah hob-nobbed with the best, or something of the sort!

Now Noah had three daughters, and they had daughters, too,
And Louis' nephew, twice removed, who happened to be
      Hugh,
Loved one of these grand-daughters, and married her,
      perchance;
So I'm distantly related to the royal line of France!

I don't want to confuse you, but my ancient pedigree
Shows that Genghis Khan and Shakespeare are related, too, to
      me.
And it wouldn't be surprising, although it's not been proved,
That Prince Charlie is my cousin, though many times
      removed!

BIRD'S NEST FOR SALE

(I've seen some odd signs as I've travelled this land, and this was one of the strangest!)

"Bird's nest for sale," - well, that's what read;
"Bird's nest for sale," - that's what the sign said.
"Bird's nest for sale," ten dollars the price,
A strange little sign, it made me look twice.

I've seen many signs on the roadside before,
And most, I'll admit, I completely ignore:
Although, now and then one catches my eye,
Like "Pinkeyes for sale", but most I pass by.

"Bird's nest for sale" - I didn't slow down,
I just kept on driving away from the town.
But I wish now I hadn't, for this sign on the tree
Has for now quite a while been puzzling me.

If I'd seen it in China I'd perhaps understand,
They sell bird's nest soup in that far-eastern land:
But this wasn't China - so what could it mean?
This sign by the roadside I'd fleetingly seen.

Was the nest artificial? Made from blankets and rugs,
And chemically treated to keep out the bugs?
Or was it a real one? Made of cobwebs and straw?
I should have gone in and then knocked on the door.

It's a pity I didn't, for I'll now never know
Why a nest was for sale; did the birds have to go?
Perhaps they migrated, flew north to be warm,
Or, maybe, their nest was blown down in a storm.

It could be an entreprenaurial child
Goes out every month to where it is wild
And gathers up nests which he's able to sell
At ten dollars a pop - he might do very well!

I guess it is legal - I'm really not sure,
I've not seen people selling such items before.
And I'll now never know what strange little tale
Was behind that odd sign saying "Bird's nest for sale!"

THE KITCHEN CABINET

(This is the story of our kitchen cabinet. It is about seventy years old, and has sliding leadlight doors, metal-lined bread bin, and one of the side panels is of metal mesh so that it could be used for storing vegetables.
An interesting piece of furniture, but it has caused me a few problems, and my wife some years of frustration!)

We've had our kitchen cabinet now for thirty years and more;
It was mother's, and she bought it back in nineteen thirty-four.
She said that we could have it - it was rather knocked about;
But we, being newly married, could make use of it, no doubt!

The handles on the cupboard doors each showed a bit of rust,
The shelving all was badly stained and inches thick in dust.
The varnish that once covered it was in a dreadful mess,
But I, being optimistic, said I'd fix it up, I guess!

It took a fair amount of time but, eventually, one night
We proudly carried it inside, now painted brilliant white.
For years it held our crockery, our vegetables and bread,
But, finally, we took it out and stored it in the shed.

We shifted house some years ago, in nineteen ninety-three:
And then my darling Yvonne, she ups and says to me,
"That cabinet that belonged to Mum, the one you painted
      white,
I reckon we could use it here, if you could make it right."

"There's nothing wrong with it," I said. But then she says to
      me,
"Our house is lined with pine throughout - I'm sure you would
      agree
That that old cabinet would look best if it was stained to
      match."
And I replied, "I'm sure it would, but there's a little catch!"

"You see, my dear, I painted it, as I can well recall,
With undercoat, and overcoat, but sealer first of all.
And now it's set as hard as rock, and I can tell you true,
To strip the paint and stain it all's a dreadful job to do!"

But, nonetheless, I started it and, every now and then,
I took a blade or scraper to the wretched paint again.
I cleaned and sanded all the wood, I fixed the leadlight doors,
And on it put three coats of stain, it took five years, and more!

I carried it into the house; it now looks pretty good;
It holds for us so many things, as all good cupboards should.
I must admit the end result was worth the sweat and pain,
But I hope, in years to come, we don't shift house again!

A SAD FAREWELL

(The little one and two-teacher rural schools, once a common and central feature in almost every small country community in our nation, are becoming more and more rare - and that, in my opinion, is a turn for the worse, not the better.)

Nearly all our tiny schools,
That kept their own regime of rules,
Have shut, or been amalgamated.
I wish they could be reinstated,
For most gave marvellous education
To the children round our nation.
But, more than that, they helped to hold
The District unity of old.
They made the children feel that they
All had a special part to play;
A sense of worth, of family, too -
I'm sad those schools are gone - aren't you?

82

PAT

(This is a story about another road sign, and I think it was even stranger than "Bird's Nest For Sale"! {p.78}
My wife and I happened to be on holiday, exploring rhis wonderful land of ours. We drove through, and stopped at, town after town, hamlet after hamlet. Each little community had something special to offer, something special to see. At one particular place we saw a sign that really intrigued us - even more so than the sign discussed in the last poem.
This is the story behind that sign.)

We found a little sleepy town, away out in the scrub,
That had, we saw, a fine hotel I'll call "The Outback Pub".
It's been a drinking hole for years for many local blokes,
And also some from out of town, the less suburban folks!

A seasoned drinker, Pat by name, lived one 'K' out of town;
He'd come there many years before, and there he settled down.
I wasn't told his stock-in-trade, or if he worked at all,
But often Pat would make, I'm told, the pub his port-of-call.

He'd wander up along the road, followed by his dog;
A faithful friend who'd sit and wait while Pat enjoyed his
      grog.
He'd have to sit a longish while for, as you've all supposed,
The usual time for Pat to leave was when the doors were
      closed.

There were some nights that Pat would be unsteady on his
      feet,
As gently he approached the steps that led him to the street;
And, on negotiating these, Pat would cheerfully roam
Wobbling, and yet unconcerned, along the road to home.

It was irrelevant to Pat that cars might use the road
That he strolled wearily along towards his own abode.
The dog ignored this fact as well, and both of them would
      head
A wavy course from from pub to home before they went to
      bed.

The locals were concerned that Pat might meet a sorry end,
If, late one night, a car should come careering round a bend
With, p'raps, a stranger driving, and completely unaware
That ageing Pat and trusty dog could easily be there.

So now a roadsign has been made in black and yellow paint,
A picture of a man and dog - it's really rather quaint!
"Caution," it reads, "Pat on road the next one 'K' or so."
And Pat and dog are still alive - as far as one can know!

GEOGRAPHY

(Schooldays, for many of us, are rapidly becoming a distant and hazy memory, and the facts and figures we once knew are long gone, lost in the cobwebs of the years!
You might remember, as I do, having to learn lists of dates, lists of rules, and lists and definitions of many geographical features, tallest mountains, longest rivers, capital cities, and so on.
This is to both remind and encourage those whose memory is not as sharp as they would wish - I know the feeling!)

Geography! Geography!
This subject always interests me.
When I was young, just seven or eight,
I had to learn about Bass Strait,
And promontories and gulfs and capes,
And what made islands different shapes.
Deltas, headlands, lakes, lagoons,
Deserts, oceans, mountains, dunes,
Volcanoes, glaciers, rivers, cirques,
In Geography we got the works!
For each of these we had to know
Examples of them each to show
That we had learnt about them all;
And we were told we should recall

The names of some of them, at least.
But as the load of terms increased,
Along with definitions, too,
Frustration of some students grew
Until they felt their brains would bust;
Some even gave up in disgust!
But me, I loved to learn each list,
And not one definition missed.
I could readily recite
Why the Great Australian Bight
Was not a gulf, or sea, or bay;
And chant, at any time of day,
The Beaufort Scale from storm to breeze,
The longest rivers, deepest seas,
Tallest mountains, biggest lakes.
Ten of each, at least, I knew,
And listed them in order, too!

That's over fifty years ago!
I, nowadays, no longer know
Those facts and figures I knew then,
And doubt I ever will again!
But will it matter overmuch
If I don't know that such and such
Is biggest, longest, most or more?
It won't mean a jot, I'm sure.
But if I want to know - I bet
They'll all be on the Internet!!!!

AN INTRODUCTION

(When performing, or giving a talk to some group or other, I often use the poem "A Healthy Lifestyle" {"Australian Poems That Would Stun A Sheep"} that I wrote some years ago.
However, that is not an accurate picture of who I am, and neither is this! But it does give, perhaps, a little insight in to the writing side of my character, at least.
Although I've been writing poetry for nearly forty years, it is only in the last ten to fifteen years that I have taken it at all seriously, and increased my output considerably!)

I'm, for better or worse,
A purveyor of verse,
A poet I am, so it's said.
I enjoy what I do
As I write something new
With the words that drift round in my head.

As I quote this or that,
I wear an old hat,
An Akubra of uncertain years.
I say them aloud,
And trust that the crowd
Appreciate all that they hear.

So what do I write
As I sit up at night
And earnestly scribble away?

What words do I find
When thoughts come to mind
At any time during the day?

I write about life,
And a beautiful wife;
Of feelings and passion and fun.
I write about grief,
Of death and belief,
My list I have hardly begun!

I write about plants,
And spiders and ants,
Of animals, harvest and grain.
I write about wealth,
Of food and of health,
Of anguish and illness and pain.

Many stories I've heard
On what has occurred
In the mountains, the bush, and the town.
And, whether they're true
Or a fantasy new,
I'm happy to write them all down.

I'm, for better or worse,
A purveyor of verse,
And I write in my own special style.
And as long as my head
Isn't damaged or dead,
I'll be writing for yet quite a while!

THE END

(What does one put on the last page of a poetry book?
Perhaps this will do!)

In an Oriental folk tale, "The Tomb of Noorsheerwan",
Haroon, who was the caliph, (now many years long gone),
Found a cave of precious treasures, and amongst them was a
     crown,
So he packed them all together, and took the lot to town.
He was a wealthy caliph, but he was a scholar, too,
He loved to search for knowledge, to discover something new.
This crown it was five-sided, and, when he had a look,
Found each side closely-written, like pages of a book.
The words were pithy sayings, were maxims old and rare,
The caliph was delighted, and he stated then and there
That all should be recorded, for, of all the treasure,
It was the words of knowledge that gave him greatest pleasure.
I haven't room to quote them, for this poem's nearly done,
But I think that I can manage to share this little one.
Haroon found it on the crown, its fifth and final side,
Its wisdom is remarkable, and cannot be denied!
These few short words were written upon the topmost line,
And, dare I say, they may be true in others lives than mine.
"Fear kings," it read, "and women," and then, this proverb old,
Concluded with, "and poets," in letters rich and bold.
Now kings are scarce at present, and rarely give a fright,
And women? They are lovely, I find them quite all right!
But poets, they're the odd ones, of them I'd steer well clear:
Of each of those fore-mentioned - the poet's the one to fear!